Our Changing Planet

LEVEL 6

Written by: Coleen Degnan-Veness
Series Editor: Melanie Williams

Pearson Education Limited
Edinburgh Gate, Harlow,
Essex CM20 2JE, England
and Associated Companies throughout the world.

ISBN: 978-1-4479-4432-4

This edition first published by Pearson Education Ltd 2013

9 10 8

Text copyright © Pearson Education Ltd 2013

The moral rights of the author have been asserted
in accordance with the Copyright Designs and Patents Act 1988

Set in 15/19pt OT Fiendstar
Printed in Great Britain by Ashford Colour Press Ltd.
SWTC/02

Acknowledgements

The publisher would like to thank the following for their kind permission to reproduce their photographs:
(Key: b-bottom; c-center; l-left; r-right; t-top)

Alamy Images: All Canada Photos 3cr, 16, 17, Mark Baigent 23, David R. Frazier Photolibrary, Inc. 25, dbimages 13, Bruce Farnsworth 28, John Glover 22 (inset), imagebroker 26, Juniors Bildarchiv GmbH 19t, Lightworks Media 11t, Jeff Rotman 18 (inset), Alex Segre 20-21, Christopher Stewart 36t, WILDLIFE GmbH 15; **Brand X Pictures:** Morey Milbradt 11br; **Corbis:** Fancy 24, Hero 25 (inset), Matthias Schrader / epa 37, Lucas Oleniuk / ZUMA Press 32, 32 (inset); **Fotolia.com:** 33, Danicek 35, Dmytro Sukharevskyy 7br, Galyna Andrushko 5b, Vlad61_61 4 (inset); **Getty Images:** AFP 8, eyeswideopen 34, Guenter Fischer 23b, Gamma-Rapho 9, Paul Paul 36b, Paul Souders 14, Dave Stamboulis Travel Photography 3l, 10, Jami Tarris 29; **John Foxx Images:** Imagestate 27b; **Pearson Education Ltd:** Oxford Designers & Illustrators Ltd 5t, 6, title page, Jules Selmes 36c; **Rex Features:** KPA / Zuma 19b; **Shutterstock.com:** 4, Anton Foltin 11cl, Olmarmar 22, Photodynamic 3cl, 30, smereka 7t, Specta 18, Wandee007 27t; The Dian Fossey Gorilla Fund International; 800 Cherokee Avenue, S.E.; Atlanta, Georgia 30315; 1-800-851-0203; www.gorillafund.org: 31; **WaterAid:** Jon Spaull 3r

Cover images: Pearson Education Ltd: *Front:* Digital Vision; *Back:* Oxford Designers & Illustrators Ltd

All other images © Pearson Education

In some instances we have been unable to trace the owners of copyright material,
and we would appreciate any information that would enable us to do so.

Illustrations: David Semple

Published by Pearson Education Ltd

For a complete list of the titles available in the Pearson English Kids Readers series, please go to
www.pearsonenglishkidsreaders.com. Alternatively, write to your local Pearson Education office or to
Pearson English Readers Marketing Department, Pearson Education, Edinburgh Gate, Harlow, Essex CM20 2JE, England.

Contents

Climate is Changing

The Earth's environments – dry deserts, icy deserts, rain forests, grasslands, mountains, and oceans – are the amazing habitats for life on this planet. The climate in each of these environments is important. But climate is changing faster than ever before, and the Earth is getting hotter. Scientists call this global warming.

Many scientists worry about the health and future of our planet. They tell us that we must change how we live. They say that we are destroying nature's habitats.

FACT

More than 1.2 million plant and animal species live on Earth.

QUESTION

What on Earth is happening?

desert a very dry land which is often sandy
global warming the result when the sun's heat cannot escape from the Earth
habitat the place where wild animals and plants live
species a group, or family, of plants or animals

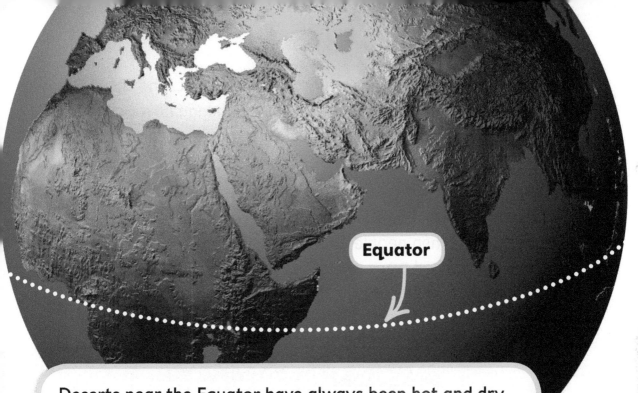

Equator

Deserts near the Equator have always been hot and dry with no more than 25 centimeters of rain each year. But the deserts are getting hotter and drier, which is bringing dangerous droughts.

To the north and south of the Equator are the tropical rain forests, which can get up to 250 centimeters of rain each year! The rain forests have more plant species than anywhere else. But we have cut down a lot of trees.

Scientists say global warming and our careless ways are threatening deserts, rain forests, and other important habitats.

QUESTION

Can *we* do something about it?

drought a long time without rain

The sun's power moves oceans around the planet, and the result is different climates. People cannot change how oceans move. But we can reduce the greenhouse gases, such as carbon dioxide and methane, in the atmosphere.

Greenhouse gases keep our planet warm, but too many make the Earth too hot. There is now more carbon dioxide in the air than ever. When people and animals breathe out carbon dioxide, plants, and trees take it in. When we destroy trees, more carbon dioxide stays in the atmosphere.

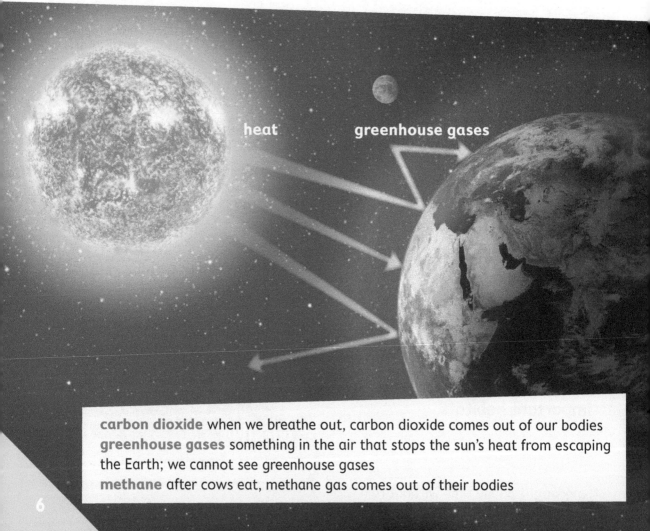

heat greenhouse gases

carbon dioxide when we breathe out, carbon dioxide comes out of our bodies
greenhouse gases something in the air that stops the sun's heat from escaping the Earth; we cannot see greenhouse gases
methane after cows eat, methane gas comes out of their bodies

When we burn fossil fuels, we produce even more carbon dioxide. Power stations and factories burn the most fossil fuels. When we drive cars or travel by plane, we burn more. Heat in our homes usually comes from burning fossil fuels, too.

Methane gas is more powerful than carbon dioxide. Farm animals' stomachs produce a lot of methane. More methane comes out of cows than out of other animals. Today, people in the richest countries eat a lot of meat so more farmers are keeping more cows.

fossil fuel something we burn, for example oil, that comes from dead plants or animals over millions of years

Droughts and Heat Waves

Scientists have found that in the past the Sahara Desert had more water. Rivers have disappeared. The result is that there is less water and food for people, plants, and animals.

In 2011, East Africa had the worst drought in 60 years. When thousands of people left their homes to look for food and water, their health became a very big problem. Thousands of young children died from diseases that are not dangerous in many other countries. Hungry children are too weak to fight disease.

QUESTION

Are droughts in Africa a result of global warming?

UNITED NATIONS CONFERENCE ON ENVIRONMENT AND DEVELOPMENT

Rio de Janeiro 3–14 June 1992

Temperatures are also rising across Europe and North America. Heat waves are not as dangerous as droughts because heat waves usually continue for no more than a week or two. But more people die from heart disease during a heat wave.

In July 2011, a large part of the US had one of the worst heat waves since 1936. In South Dakota, around 1,500 cows died.

It seems that the scientists are right about global warming. The leaders of many countries have made important changes to fight climate change since 1992.

More than 35,000 people died in Europe's heat wave in August 2003.

Hot Deserts

Hot, dry deserts cover about 20 percent of Earth's land, and they are the habitat for some amazing animals. Some desert animals can live without food and water for days. Camels can go without water for weeks!

The wild Bactrian camel in the Gobi Desert can live for months without water! But they are an endangered species because people hunt them for food and for their fur. Scientists worry that they could become extinct.

FACT
A large, thirsty camel can drink more than 150 liters in one drink.

FACT

Water is a big problem in most desert cities.

Many desert plants live for hundreds of years. Some even live without water for years! Other desert plants keep water inside their leaves for a long time.

In places where people have brought rivers to the desert, nature has come alive! Engineers discovered a way to bring the Colorado River to the desert in the American southwest. In the desert city of Phoenix, Arizona, you can see beautiful green grass, trees, and flowers. But the desert is not their natural habitat, and so they need a lot of water.

People who live in deserts, both rich and poor, need clean water. For poor people, it is difficult to find. In West Africa, many children walk for hours every day to get water for their families.

Many people in richer countries give money to help poorer people who live in deserts. The money helps to discover water deep underground and to bring it up. It also pays for toilets, which are important for people's health. Richer countries have agreed to give more money to help poorer countries.

QUESTION

Why is it important for this help to continue?

FACT

More than one billion people live in deserts.

Oceans cover 70 percent of the Earth, but plants, animals, and people cannot drink saltwater. In Kuwait, they have built factories that can take the salt out of seawater. Then, people can drink it. Some other countries in the Middle East have also built these factories. Spain and the US are now cleaning their saltwater, too.

There is one big problem — these factories use a lot of energy.

FACT

In 2011, there were 15,180 factories in 150 countries that produced clean water for 300 million people!

energy power that moves machines or makes heat

Icy Deserts

The Arctic and Antarctica are amazing icy deserts. But global warming is melting some of the ice faster than ever before. Antarctica is land covered in ice with oceans around it. It is the habitat for whales and penguins.

The Arctic is an icy ocean with land around it. It has many more animal and plant species than Antarctica. It is the habitat for whales, Polar bears, and other smaller animals. When some of the ice melts every summer, more than 1,000 species of plants come alive.

FACT

Antarctica holds about 90 percent of the Earth's ice.

FACT

The Inuit have lived in the Arctic for more than 4,000 years.

In the past, the Inuit lived very differently from the rest of the world, and their way of life did not threaten their habitat. But today, they, too, are burning more fossil fuels for heat in their modern homes and for driving.

Some scientists say that the melting ice may destroy coastal towns and cities. By the end of this century, oceans may rise by one meter. But not all scientists agree.

In the Canadian Arctic, 25 percent of Polar bears have disappeared in the last 20 years.

Scientists *do* agree that global warming is destroying the Polar bear's habitat. Polar bears hunt for animals under the ice. Less ice means less food for the bears. From late winter until April, the female bears stay under the snow with their new babies. When they come out, they are very hungry. If they cannot find enough food, they will look for it in towns. People are afraid of these fierce animals and sometimes shoot them. They are a threatened species.

Polar bears have another enemy – the oil business. After businessmen discovered oil in Alaska and Siberia, they built factories, roads, and towns. They brought jobs, which helped a lot of people. But is oil for people's homes and cars more important than protecting wildlife?

Scientists are working hard to save the Polar bear. They have put radios around the necks of some bears so they can follow them. As a result, scientists can learn more about them. They can see where the bears are finding food. Sadly they have discovered that the bears have to travel far to find food.

Marine Life

Global warming and pollution endanger marine life, too. For 200 years, people have produced too much carbon dioxide, and about half of it has gone into seas and oceans. As a result, the water has changed. We can see for ourselves that the colorful coral on the Great Barrier Reef in Australia, and in other places, has turned white. This means that the coral is dying.

The oceans are getting too warm for coral, which is the habitat for many other small marine species. So they are dying, too. Scientists are working hard to protect them.

coral the bodies of millions of very small animals that built homes on rock in warm water for over 200 million years
marine from the sea or ocean

Since the 1970s, many countries have worked with scientists to protect dolphins, but this intelligent species is not free from danger. In South America, fishermen kill the pink Amazon River dolphin because it eats a large number of fish. This means less fish for the fishermen.

Killer whales, the world's largest dolphins, live in all of the oceans from the Arctic to Antarctica. They enjoy playing with people and solving problems so many sealife parks like to show them off to their visitors.

QUESTION

Is it right to take Killer whales out of their habitat and keep them in pools?

It is good for our health to eat less meat and eat more fish. In Asia, people eat a lot of fish, and they seem to have fewer diseases than meat-eaters in the West.

Some fish are becoming dangerously threatened because fishermen are catching too many of one kind of fish. People should eat more different kinds of fish so the popular fish do not become extinct.

Many countries are now working together to protect marine species. They have agreed on the number of fish each country can catch.

QUESTION

Do you eat different kinds of fish?

Large numbers of people live around the Mediterranean Sea. Many of the most endangered species of marine life live in very deep water there. Countries around the Mediterranean have agreed to stop catching fish from deeper than 1,000 meters.

There is protection for 18 species of whales, dolphins, and other sea animals in a part of the Mediterranean Sea, but this covers only about one percent of the sea. There are plans to protect more of it in future.

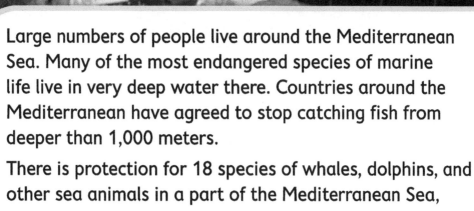

EUROPE

AFRICA

Mediterranean Sea

FACT

The Mediterranean coast is 46,000 kilometers long, and the sea is the most threatened sea in the world.

Saving Water

It is very important that we use water wisely. Think about your family's use of water. Do you take baths or short showers? Do you keep the water on when you brush your teeth? When you drink water, do you fill the glass and drink only a half of it? Does your family wash clothes in a machine that is only half full? Does your family save rain water for your garden?

FACT

The bathroom is where people use the most water inside their houses.

FACT

In the US, each person uses about 800 liters of water every day. In parts of Africa, each person uses only 22 liters.

Earth's water is for everyone, but some people use much more water than other people. When people eat cow's meat, they are using water. This may sound strange, but it takes a lot of water to grow grass for cows! Eating chickens or sheep is better for our planet because they do not need as much water as cows.

It is necessary to reduce how much water we use.

QUESTION

Do you eat meat? How much?

Reduce, Reuse, Recycle

Many people buy things and then throw them away soon after. Our trash is polluting our environment.

QUESTION

Can we reduce the mountains of trash in our cities and towns?

We should also reduce how much fuel we use.

QUESTION

Can I walk or ride my bicycle to school? Do I *need* to go by car?

We should reuse things, too.

QUESTION

Do I throw away a plastic sandwich bag every day? Could I use a lunchbox?

We can recycle paper, glass, and plastic and reduce these mountains of trash!

REDUCE

✔ When it is possible, drink the water in your kitchen. Do not buy water from the supermarket.

✔ Buy less food in packages that you will throw away.

✔ Buy less food. It is better to shop more often and to buy less.

✔ Buy only the clothes you need.

REUSE

✔ Make birthday cards and gifts from things you have at home.

RECYCLE

✔ Buy recycled wood furniture – and save our forests!

Tropical Rain Forests

Tropical rain forests are alive with insects, snakes, monkeys, birds, frogs, and many other animals. The climate is wet and warm all year so the rain forests are the perfect habitat for millions of species of plants, too.

Rain forests cover about six percent of Earth's land. They are very important because they produce oxygen and use carbon dioxide. But some countries have lost as much as 80 percent of their rain forests.

FACT

About one-quarter of the world's medicines come from rain forest plants.

oxygen when we breathe in, we breathe in oxygen

QUESTION

Why are people cutting down these amazing forests?

Farmers in Malaysia and Indonesia have cut down large parts of their amazing rain forests to grow a plant that produces a cooking oil. Farmers in other countries have cut down trees to grow bananas and other tropical fruit, which they sell around the world. With the money they get, they feed their own families.

Millions of people live in rain forests, and they burn wood for heat. They also use wood for furniture, which they sell around the world.

QUESTION

How can we stop people from destroying the rain forests?

Rain forest children live differently from other children. They do not have TVs or computers, and their parents do not have cars. Some children go to school, but other children do not. Their parents and neighbors teach them how to hunt, get water from the river, and cut firewood. Some children help grow fruits and vegetables in the family's garden.

Of course, rain forest families do not want their homes to disappear. But many of them have had to move to towns and cities because businessmen have taken their land.

Many people around the world want to protect the rain forests. Their message is clear –

- Rain forest families must be able to stay in the forests. They know more than scientists about the rain forest plants and animals. If we lose these people, we will lose a lot of information.

- People must stop buying rain forest animals for pets.

- People must stop buying animal body parts for medicine.

- People should not buy furniture made of rain forest wood from Asia, South America, or Africa.

FACT

People hunt Bengal tigers because they can sell their body parts for medicine.

29

Saving Mountain Gorillas

When we watch nature shows on TV, we learn a lot about wild animals. We know, for example, that African Mountain gorillas live in groups and that they eat forest plants and some insects. The most important male gorilla is the father of most of the babies. He leads the group through the forest, looking for food every day.

The female gorillas become mothers around the age of ten, and they keep their babies close to them for about four years.

We know about Mountain gorillas because of one brave woman's hard work.

In the 1960s, an American woman, Dian Fossey, went to the Virunga Volcano Mountains in Rwanda to study gorillas. She watched them carefully and wrote about their family groups. Dian became famous around the world when she stopped people from stealing and hunting the gorillas.

Many people have continued Dian's work. They study the gorillas and keep information about their health.

They notice changes, for example when one gorilla has died and another is born. This information helps to protect the species from extinction.

Gorillas in Democratic Republic of Congo are still endangered. Men destroyed much of their habitat with big machines after they discovered coltan underground there. Many gorillas died. In the early 2000s, those men got a lot of money for coltan from makers of cell phones.

Recycling cell phones helps save gorillas. In 2008, an eight-year-old American, Mariah Nablo, decided to help after she noticed a recycling box at the zoo. Mariah put recycling boxes in buildings around her town.

FACT

In 2011, Mariah had 1,785 cell phones for recycling.

coltan a black metal underground

Gorillas still have enemies, and man is their worst enemy. Some men hunt gorillas so they can sell their body parts. Some men take baby gorillas from their mothers to sell them. Many gorillas have died from diseases brought into the forests by man.

But there is good news. Between 1989 and 2003, the number of gorillas in the Virunga Mountains grew by 17 percent. By 2010, the number grew by another nine percent. People *can* save forests and the animals in them!

FACT

The Mountain gorilla is still an endangered species with only about 800 alive today.

Reducing Pollution

When people throw things away, for example mobile phones, TVs, and computers, they need to be sensible. People should ask themselves, "Is it possible to fix it? Do I need a new machine?" We can save energy and reduce pollution if we buy fewer machines. Or we can buy machines that are not as bad for the environment. Scientists are always working on ideas for better machines that use less energy and fossil fuels. It is possible to buy washing machines, for example, that use less energy.

FACT

Some trash is dangerous and pollutes land and water.

When we burn fossil fuels, we pollute the air. A lot of people in the world today have breathing problems because there is too much air pollution from factories, cars, and planes. It is not a surprise that city air smells differently from air in the country.

When this pollution mixes with rain, the rain becomes dangerous for plant and marine life. It can even destroy rock! Scientists have found that this rain makes some forests grow more slowly. And some forests are dying.

Since the 1970s, scientists have helped countries to reduce this environmental problem.

Children can make a Difference

Did you know that there are things YOU can do at home to help protect our planet?

You can begin by saving energy.

✔ Turn off the lights when you leave a room.
✔ Turn off your computer and TV and play outside.
✔ Turn off your radio when you are not listening to it.

You can ask your parents to do these things at home.

✔ Reduce the temperature in your house in cold countries.
✔ Wash clothes only when they are dirty. Dry them outside.
✔ Do not always use machines to clean floors.

You can help the environment in other ways, too! At school, perhaps your class can plant a tree or a wildlife garden that will invite insects and birds.

In 2007, Felix Finkbeiner, at the age of nine, decided to plant one million trees in Germany. He talked about it in his school, and people liked his idea. After three years, there were one million more trees in Germany. His idea is "Plant for the Planet", and Felix is now famous all over the world.

So you see, it is possible for children to make a difference!

Fourteen ways that you can help our planet

1 Eat less meat from cows.

2 Eat different kinds of fish.

3 Save water.

4 Use less energy at home.

5 Shop sensibly.

6 Walk or ride your bicycle when possible.

7 Recycle your trash.

8 Reduce – buy less food and fewer clothes.

9 Reuse – make birthday presents.

10 Give money to people in poorer countries.

11 Plant a tree.

12 Join or start an environmental group.

13 Read more about Earth's amazing environments.

14 Tell everyone what on Earth is happening!

Activity page 1

Before You Read

1 **Find the words below in your dictionary.
Then find pictures in the book.**

a dry desert   a Polar bear

the Equator   coral

a drought   recycling

greenhouse gases   gorillas

a camel   trash

2 **Look at the cover of the book. Read the Contents page
and look at the pictures.**

a What do you think the book is about? Why?

b What animals do you think you will read about?

c What people do you think you will read about?

3 **Look at the pictures on the pages in brackets. Answer the
question about each picture.**

a Why is rain important? (page 5)

b Can world leaders do anything for the environment? (page 9)

c Where is the boy? What is he doing? Why? (page 12)

d Where do you think these people live? How is their life
different than yours? (page 15)

Activity page 2

After You Read

1 **Read and write True (T) or False (F).**

a People and animals can drink saltwater.

b The Arctic is the habitat for whales, Polar bears, and people.

c Ice in the Arctic and Antarctica is melting because of global warming.

d The Arctic Polar bear is not a threatened species.

e Global warming and pollution are endangering marine life, for example coral.

2 **Answer the questions.**

a What is happening to the pink Amazon River dolphin? Why?

b What will happen if people do not eat different kinds of fish?

c Why is it better for the environment if people eat more meat from chickens and sheep, and less from cows?

d How can we help to protect the rain forests?

3 **Copy the map on to a piece of paper. Label the map with the names below.**

> South America   Africa   Europe
> Equator   North America   Asia
> Australia   Antarctica   the Arctic